Steve —

Thank you for making a difference with our youth.

You rock!!

Chase your dreams!

— PL

Copyright © 2018 by Jostens, Inc.

ISBN 978-0-9993306-2-3

Published by
Jostens, Inc.
7760 France Avenue South, #400
Minneapolis, MN 55435

JostensRenaissance.com

Cover photo by Danish Nelson.
Artwork by Trey Locke.

I know Phil Campbell and respect his work a great deal; however, this book took that respect to a whole new level. As he shared his own story, I discovered new ways to reach students who often give up on themselves. The humility and vulnerability that PC shares in this book make it safe for me to acknowledge my own mistakes in trying to reach students who are facing a multitude of challenges. The ideas and tools Phil shares are such an encouragement to continue to reach for these students and give them "my best." By the end of the book, I felt so ready to use my own moments of vulnerability to reach students of all backgrounds and encourage them to reach for "their best!"

– Phil Boyte, Link Crew Creator, Speaker and Consultant

In *I See You, I Hear You, & I Love You*, PC shows how he is a master of connecting with kids and adults alike. This book reads like a conversation with him and inspires the reader to be a better leader, educator, and person. Working with at-risk youth can be a challenge, but that's what we as educators really signed up for, isn't it? Every single day we are given the opportunity to impact the life of a child. As PC says, "how do you NOT do it?" A great, fast read by an awesome educator and human being. Thank you PC for sharing your heart and your passion.

– Darrin M. Peppard, Ed. D., Jostens Renaissance Educator of the Year 2015

Contents

Dedication 3

Foreword 4

Part I: Unloved 6

    This section chronicles PC's personal life journey and illustrates the struggles that many of our nation's youth face on a daily basis.

Part II: Shifting Tides 12

    Follow PC's evolution as an educator, from being a stereotypical coach to a loving, caring classroom teacher.

Part III: My Kids 17

    Take a look inside the stories of some of the most influential kids and their lasting impact on this educator's career.

Part IV: See, Hear, Love 37

    Explore ideas and tips for improving culture and climate from both a school-wide perspective and an individual classroom perspective.

Part V: Reflections 53

    This section challenges you to self-evaluate your personal thoughts and beliefs to create a deeper sense of understanding of both yourself and your life's purpose as a leader.

About the Author 70

Dedication

My goals in writing this book are twofold:

1. To help fund projects for at-risk students and their families.

2. To provide an educational resource that will aid educators in better relating to their students in hopes of providing them with the hope of a better tomorrow.

Through my partnership with Jostens, I am honored to say that 100% of the profits from every sale of this book will be donated to Chase Your Dreams Foundation, a nonprofit designed to directly benefit at-risk youth and their families.

This book is essentially my heart on paper. I hope that sharing my personal journey will ignite a spark that helps you in your quest to make our world a better place as well.

This book is dedicated to the memory of Jon Ferrell. I love you, little buddy.

PC

Foreword

It was one of the most difficult summers of my life so far. Granted, I was only 13 years old at the time, but it was tough nonetheless. My father's company transferred him from the state of Maryland, which I had called home for nearly my entire life, and he picked our family up and moved us across the country to Southern California. Now I am not sure if there is ever a good time to do this to an adolescent boy on the cusp of the most awkward few years of his life, but to me, this wasn't it. There was very little positive on the horizon for me.

When I stepped on the campus of Buena High School in Ventura, it was as if I were a ghost that no one could see. I was shy and lacked the self-confidence that I had back "home" in Maryland. I spent the first two or three weeks eating alone in the cafeteria, walking from class to class trying to figure out how to convince my parents that it would be a wise financial move for my Dad to quit his job so we could go back where we all knew we belonged.

That changed when two people made a concerted effort to take me out of the self-imposed shadows I was traveling in and include me in their daily lives. Lori and Kevin independently introduced me to their friend groups and more important, took an honest interest in me and who I was as a person. They were my first two California friends, and in many ways, they saved me.

That was many years ago. I now spend my days as a classroom teacher and recently celebrated my 22nd year in the most noble of professions. I have committed my life and my calling to make sure that kids are not invisible on our campus and that we create a culture where everyone feels they have a place in our world.

Jostens Renaissance is a program that is also committed to helping schools create cultures that embrace the entire school community. I have had the honor and the privilege to work with this organization for 10 years now, and it was at a Jostens Renaissance National Conference that I first met Dr. Phil Campbell for the first time. We immediately connected on a deep level as we quickly realized our shared passion for making a positive impact on the lives of students, not just in our own schools but in the lives of kids all over this country.

PC is a man of many talents, but without a doubt his greatest asset is the heart that beats within his chest. He has a heart for kids, and more specifically, kids who have been labeled for decades in our profession as "at-risk." The book that you are holding right now is a sample of the passion that oozes out of Phil. You are about to take a journey with him as he shares his heart and his mind for these kids and will give you practical ideas and tools that you can apply today in your school.

The title of this book, *I See You, I Hear You, & I Love You*, are not just words. Phil Campbell means them every single time he says them. It is my hope that you embrace this mantra in your school and in your life as well. Join us in being agents of change in your school and in our world.

Paul Dols, 2018 Jostens Renaissance Hall of Fame

Part I: Unloved

I was adopted when I was in the 7th grade. My last name changed from Kenney to Campbell. As a 12-year-old boy, I didn't view this moment as being a big deal at the time. In all honesty, it was only important to my mom and not really a big concern to me.

I can still vividly recall my last encounter with my dad prior to my adoption. While I lived and grew up in Tennessee, my dad lived in Texas. I would get to visit him once or twice a year. My favorite part of my visits was that I got to fly to and from Texas all by myself. Because of that, I got first-class treatment from all of the flight attendants and I even got to visit the captain in the cockpit prior to most of my flights taking off.

This was prior to the 9/11 attacks, so security was quite different at the time. People could walk all the way down to the departure gates at the airport, regardless of whether they had a flight or not. I can remember sitting just inside the airport departure gate, squatting along with my dad. He said to me, "No matter what you decide about changing your last name, I will always be your dad, and I will always love you."

Based on that information, the adoption was processed and my life would remain unchanged. Or so I thought. My next time period to visit my dad came and went without any contact from him. Then, Christmas came and went. And then, my birthday came and went, all without a word from my dad. For four years, my dad completely disappeared.

I don't have the words to accurately describe how it feels to be unloved. Lost. Insecure. Hopeless. Defeated. Worthless. That's a shot in the dark at the feeling. The vast majority of us, myself included, take love for granted, because we've never been forced to exist in a life without it. But just for a minute, close your eyes and imagine yourself in a world where love doesn't exist, where you are seen as more of an inconvenience than a son or daughter, and where the boundaries of humanity cease to exist.

It's a hollow, harrowing sense to even think about it, isn't it?

Now, close your eyes again, and this time, think about students you have had in class that have endured similar circumstances. Think to yourself what it is that they go home to, what it is that they wake up to, and what it is that they are exposed to in their home and surrounding neighborhood. So many, too many, of our youth exist in a world without love.

But together, you and me, we're gonna change that.

I am happy to say that today, my relationship with my dad has been repaired and is in a much better place. But for those four years, as a young, impressionable teenager, I was mad. I was angry. I felt lost, worthless, and defeated. Arguably more than anything else, I felt lied to. If your own dad can turn his back on you and essentially forget your existence, who can you trust in this world? More important, HOW can you trust in this world? And is love even a real thing?

I can't help but wonder if many of our at-risk youth experience these same emotions and ask themselves these same questions.

[
They aren't labeled as "at-risk" based on their human potential; they are labeled based on extenuating circumstances of which they had absolutely no control.
]

Adoption was and still is MY struggle. Unfortunately, that doesn't even scratch the surface of what many of our youth have to face and fight to overcome in their personal lives.

I was fortunate to have three rocks in my life: my mom, my stepfather that adopted me who I call dad, and the game of baseball.

For the vast majority of my life, baseball was my safe place. One of my earliest memories is my first baseball game that I ever played. I was 5 years old and a member of the Cubs, coached by a man named Don Davis. Still to this day, Mr. Davis coaches in youth leagues in my hometown and always wears his signature sleeveless shirts in the process. I was playing first base that day, and with a runner on first, the batter hit a line drive in my direction. I dove and caught the ball, got up, and ran to tag first base to double up the base runner that didn't understand what it meant to "tag up." Double play. My first phone call when I got home was to my Grandma in Illinois and I was so excited to tell her my big news!

Regardless of what was going on in my life, stepping onto the baseball field was always a release for me. As I got older and had to deal with the "stress" of school, girls, and being a teenager, baseball was my outlet. No matter what was going on in life, nothing could touch me or impact me on the baseball field. I was in my element and life couldn't get in my way or slow me down.

I grew up in my hometown of Murfreesboro, Tennessee, home of Middle Tennessee State University. I grew up attending baseball games at MTSU and absolutely worshiped the ground those guys walked on. I even took hitting lessons with some of the MTSU coaches and I can still remember the amazement on my face the first time they took me into the players' locker room. It didn't take many trips to the park to watch those guys play ball for a dream to develop: I wanted to play baseball at MTSU for head coach Steve Peterson.

The only problem I ran into in pursuing this dream was that I was 5'7" and 135 pounds soaking wet. On top of that, a knee surgery took away one of my biggest threats that I had on the baseball field: speed. I was an above-average high school baseball player and one of the premier players on my team and in our district, but I wasn't great by any stretch of the imagination. By the time my senior year was underway, I had exactly zero offers from junior colleges or universities to play college baseball.

Essentially, nobody wanted me.

Take a second to consider how many of our students feel the exact same way, except on a much larger scale. In the grand scheme of things, not receiving an offer to play college baseball is grossly trivial compared to a child enduring a life of abandonment. A life of bouncing from foster home to foster home. A life of poverty and inconceivable living conditions. A life of drugs, hatred, and abuse. A life without love.

I have so many stories, some of which I will share in this book, of hardships that students have had to endure. Many people often stress empathy as a key trait in today's society, but the truth is, I cannot begin to fathom many of the experiences that my kids have seen. In a world where we all believe that our own personal struggles are all that matter, the truth is that many of our nation's youth have endured and are enduring struggles beyond our comprehension.

[*While I can't step into their shoes to endure their pain and suffering, nor in all reality do I want to, I CAN do one thing: I can love them. And I do.*]

In the fall of 1997, I stepped foot onto Reese Smith Field as an uninvited walk-on for the MTSU baseball team. I can vividly remember parking in the parking lot and seeing Kyle Thomas, a catcher that just graduated from another high school in town who had received a scholarship to play baseball at MTSU. I wished with all my heart that I was as good as Kyle Thomas that day.

I can remember stepping to the gate down the right field line to enter the field. Most of the team was already on the field, taking batting practice prior to the official start of practice. They all had on white pants, blue MTSU baseball tops, and blue caps with the MT logo on them. There I stood, dressed in high school summer baseball gear, with an overwhelming sense of fear and self-doubt that I had never felt in my entire life. There were guys on that field that as recently as the previous season, I had sat in the stands and watched in wonder and admiration of their skill sets.

I poured every ounce of everything I had onto that field that day. So much so that after practice when I returned to my Jeep, which was a 5-speed, I literally couldn't push the clutch in with my left leg to get it started. But, more important, I didn't hear my last name called by Coach Pete at the end of practice that day, because that meant you were getting cut. I survived to see tomorrow.

I worked harder that fall than I had ever worked for anything in my entire life. I didn't have the size. I didn't have the speed. I didn't have the power. Simply put, I didn't have the skills to play at that level. But I had the heart. I had the drive. I had the work ethic. I had the relentless passion to work myself to the point of exhaustion each and every single day to make my dream come true.

Finally, the head assistant coach, Jim McGuire, asked me to follow him up to the press box after practice one day late that fall. I knew that Coach Pete had done all of the cuts up until that point, but I still wasn't sure why Mags had asked me to follow him. Was he taking me to have a private conversation to break the bad news? Had I done something wrong? I literally had no idea what was taking place.

When we got to the press box, he explained that they were out of the regular MTSU practice jerseys, so this would have to do. He reached into a box and pulled out a blue shirt that said 'MTSU Baseball' on the front and had the number 5 on the back and handed it to me. I made it all the way to my vehicle without breaking down, and then proceeded to cry uncontrollably the entire way home. Once I got home and told my parents the big news, I picked up the phone and made the same excited phone call that I did 13 years earlier to that same special person in Illinois: my Grandma.

Part II: Shifting Tides

I entered the teaching profession based not on a love of teaching, but instead on a love of coaching. Having graduated college with a degree in agriculture, I quickly realized that I would have trouble getting a job in that career field due to my lack of real-world farming experience. Instead, I found work at a vehicle manufacturing facility that I affectionately referred to as "The Dungeon." The monotony of factory work is simply not for me, so I was quick to begin searching for an alternative means of income.

Around about this same time, a buddy of mine who was the head baseball coach at a local high school asked me to coach his fall baseball team. He promised me $500 in exchange for coaching 10 games that fall. In my mind, I had just won the lottery! Could it get any easier than coaching a few games and making what seemed like a good chunk of change at the time to a 22-year-old kid?

I set out coaching that fall with the simple intention of making an easy $500. In the process, however, I fell in love with those kids and with coaching. I decided that I would go back to school to earn my Master's Degree so that I could teach and, more specifically, so that I could coach baseball.

I graduated with my teaching certification on a Saturday in August in the summer of 2005 and started my first teaching job on the Monday immediately after at the most affluent school in my hometown. While I took my job in the classroom seriously, in all honesty, I was largely your stereotypical coach. I told my kids on the first day of each semester, "I'm not here to be your friend. I'm here to do a job and then to step on a baseball field in the afternoon." Great teacher, right?

In my early days as an educator, I was all about discipline. I wore a shirt and tie and fancy shoes to school every day because, to my understanding up to that point in my career, that helped with classroom management. I operated a tight ship with regard to tardies, makeup policies, cell phone use, and the like. At the beginning of each semester, I eagerly anticipated the first student to rebuke my authority because then I could make an example of them for all to see. No one, and I mean no one, was going to pull any funny business in my classroom and get away with it. If nothing else, those kids were going to know who was in charge.

With regard to instruction, I had a structured methodology for that as well. Students would read a chapter in the book and answer the questions and define key terminology at the end of that chapter on day 1, listen to me ramble through a brief lecture accompanied by a clipart-filled PowerPoint and fill in the blanks to an outline on day 2, and then repeat this process for the next few chapters until it was time to take a unit exam.

As I reflect on those days, I was a horrible teacher. Period.

After a few years of teaching and coaching at the high school level, I had the opportunity to coach baseball at the collegiate level. This was an amazingly fun experience. All I had to do was recruit, mow the field, and coach baseball. Does it get any better than that? A few years into my collegiate coaching tenure, however, my son, Brooks, was born. Having friends that grew up with their dads coaching college baseball and listening to their stories of the time they missed with him not being at home, I decided it was time to leave coaching so I could focus my time and efforts on being a dad. So, at this point in my career, I became "just a teacher."

In 2010, I accepted a teaching position at my bride's alma mater in Portland, TN. Portland is a small, rural town, much different than my hometown of Murfreesboro, and night and day different from my first high school teaching job. The majority of the students at Portland qualified as socioeconomically disadvantaged, rode the bus to and from school, and many were from broken homes. The environment within the high school was toxic at best. We had fights every other day, sometimes more frequently than that. There was a time that I was breaking up a fight and one of the kids turned around and tried to fight me. "What the hell have I gotten myself into?" I can remember thinking.

To make matters worse, as the new teacher and the "low man on the totem pole," I was rewarded with teaching a class called Success 101. This course was a requirement for all freshmen, yes, freshmen, to take each year in an effort to acclimate them for their high school experience, offer college and career exploration and guidance, and ease in their transition from middle school to high school. The only problem, as most high school educators have likely already pondered, was that when you put 30-35 freshmen in one room, it's a disaster waiting to happen. Combine that with an educator who has no clue what they are doing, and it's the perfect storm for failure.

To further compound the situation, Success 101 did not have a curriculum. It did not have a textbook. It did not have standards. Essentially, it was a concept that sounded like a great idea initially but received very little support in the form of structure or educational resources and supplies.

So, there I was, in a town where I didn't want to live, in a school where I didn't want to work, with a demographic and age group of students that I didn't want to teach, and with a course load that required me, a baseball coach who was no longer coaching, to create virtually every lesson from scratch.

I was mad. I was angry. I was frustrated. I was desperate. I was lost. I was hopeless.

One class in particular stands out from that first semester. It was the last class of the day (of course!) and it was the worst class I have ever taught. Every day was a battle. They came in with a mission of creating as much chaos as possible and I came in with a mission of making an example out of every single one of them. It was a tireless cycle of an out-of-touch educator attempting to "break" a group of 14-year-old teenagers.

I can't tell you how many times I debated turning in my keys and quitting during the middle of that school year. There were times when I was so frustrated during conversations at home with my bride about it that she would tell me to simply turn in my keys and walk away…it was, without question, one of the single worst experiences of my entire life.

For some reason, though, I couldn't quit.

So, I convinced myself to finish the school year in that horrible environment. My bride, who is a phenomenal educator and taught in the same building, played a major role in designing lessons and activities that I could use for those kids. Every day, I entered the battlefield with a plan of attack and simply hoped and prayed that the kids would just play along until the bell rang.

And then, slowly, almost magically really, the tide began to turn for me. I can't pinpoint a single event or activity that served as the tipping point. There wasn't a revolutionary conversation or piece of advice that led to the transformation.

But, for the first time in my teaching career, I decided to treat those kids like they were *my kids*. I decided to treat them just like I treated my baseball players as a coach.

> *For the first time in my educational career, I totally and completely let my guard down, opened my heart, and started loving those kids. And then, a funny thing happened…they started loving me back.*

And the rest, as they say, is history.

Austin. Juan. Melinda. Jeanna. Cody. Jordan. Colby. Paige. Bryson. I will never forget the names of those kids who were in that class that semester. Most of them have no idea of the impact they made on me and my career. But, if not for that group of heathens, you wouldn't be reading this right now.

Part III: My Kids

One of the most prominent theories with regard to understanding people is Maslow's Hierarchy of Needs. Our core physical and safety needs have to be satisfied before we can attempt to fulfill our emotional and psychological needs. As leaders, we don't always have the means or resources to satisfy or impact the core needs of others, but we all have the ability to care and to make a difference.

I see you. I hear you. I love you.

As human beings, we ALL have an innate need to not only *hear* those three statements, but to *feel* those three statements...to *experience* them, to truly *know* them, and to own the sense of security that they bring to our lives. Great leaders understand this and have an uncanny knack for making everyone they interact with feel like they are the most important person on the planet in that moment in time.

The transformation for me, as a leader, an educator, and as a person, took place when I completely and unconditionally invested myself in others, when I opened my heart and began to genuinely care, and when I began to empathize.

The transformation for me took place when I decided to see my kids, to hear my kids, and to love my kids. Every. Single. Day.

How many students in your building, how many adults in your building, how many people that you interact with in general, feel totally and completely invisible? How many of them feel like no one listens to their ideas or opinions? How many of them have absolutely no idea what it means to feel appreciated, to feel cared for, or to feel a sense of belonging? So many people, too many people in all honesty, are dying, sometimes literally, because they believe that they are invisible.

You and I, though, we have the power to change that with nine simple words:

I see you. I hear you. I love you.

Great leaders are more concerned with seeing others than with being seen.

Great leaders are more concerned with listening to others than with being heard.

Great leaders are more concerned with loving others than with being loved.

> *In today's society of self-centered egotism, the silver bullet we are all seeking for success in leadership lies not in our desire to attract the glow of the spotlight, but instead in our ability to direct the spotlight toward those around us.*

Leadership can never be about "me;" leadership is always about serving those around us. Leadership is about seeing, hearing, and loving.

The students in the upcoming stories document some of my personal experiences with youth. Each of these kids played a role in shaping me into the educator and, more important, into the person that I am today. I didn't "win" with every single one of these kids, but each and every single one of them made a lasting impact on my mentality toward education and mankind in general. Hopefully, at least one or two of them will trigger a connection between you and students in your building as well.

Malik

Malik was one of the first students I ever had in my first semester of teaching. He was in my business management class and sat toward the back of the room on the first day of school. That, in and of itself, was an immediate red flag for this discipline-focused newbie.

Malik was an African-American young man. He sagged his pants. He ran with a "rough crowd" of kids. During hall duty between classes, I always watch how kids interact with one another and who runs with whom...you can learn a lot about your kids between classes. While Malik was never an instigator or really even a participant in troublesome situations, he was never far from the center of the action. His group of friends was always one that you would keep an eye on, because inevitably, they were up to no good.

I stereotyped Malik.

Beyond a shadow of a doubt, completely and whole-heartedly, I 100% stereotyped this young man from the second he walked into my classroom with a comb interwoven in his hair. In my mind during those first days of school, he was going to be my example. It was just a matter of time before he was going to act out and I could punish him and embarrass him for being the "bad kid" that he was.

My opportunity never came.

As we completed a review session prior to our first exam in that class, I decided that I would test Malik and call on him to give me an answer. He got it right, along with every other time I called on him that day. He then proceeded to score one of the highest grades in the class on that exam and every one thereafter. Malik turned out to be one of the brightest kids that I have ever taught.

Later that semester, I apologized to Malik face to face. I told him that I stereotyped him before he ever even said a word based on his appearance and the group of people that he ran with. I told him that I was proud of him and explained to him how much potential he had to go places in life. Most important, I thanked him for opening my eyes to my own weakness of a lack of perspective and understanding.

Jeffery

Jeffery was a student who was borderline special needs that I taught in one of my first two years of teaching. He was enrolled in my keyboarding class. Keyboarding, in all honesty, is arguably the easiest course a high school student will ever take. All they have to do is type and they will be successful!

Jeffery sat in the back of the room at a table by himself. As I would walk around the room to monitor the students, I could always tell that Jeffery would scramble to use his mouse to change the screen on his computer as I approached. He was always typing, but somehow, he was never finishing the lessons that he was assigned for credit.

Using the software program on my teacher computer, I could monitor all of the screens that my students were using. On Jeffery's, I saw that he was diligently working on writing a story in a Word document about Pokémon. As I would stand up and walk around the room, he would minimize his story and act as if he were typing his assigned lesson for the day.

I begged Jeffery to complete his lessons. I pleaded with him. I promised him "free time" on the computer to write his story if he would just complete his lessons. Nothing worked.

Then, I had an idea. For whatever reason, I had two unopened packs of Pokémon cards at my house. I brought them to school and showed them to Jeffery. His eyes lit up, much to my liking. I promised him both packs of cards if he would simply complete his assigned lessons. That kid typed like there was no tomorrow!

Jeffery helped me realize a couple of things. One, knowing what and who your students like plays a key role in getting them to work for you. And two, as long as he was typing and getting better at using the computer, why did it matter if he was typing his own personal story or the boring, monotonous lessons I assigned to my students? This concept didn't fully sink in for me until later down the road, as we will discuss in a later chapter on instructional methods.

[*Knowing what and who your students like plays a key role in getting them to work for you.*]

Brad

I never had Brad in class. In fact, the only reason I really even knew Brad was because he dated a young lady, Samantha, who was in my class. As many high school boys do, Brad would escort Samantha to and from all of her classes, often at the expense of being late to his own.

Brad was a young man who, for all intents and purposes, didn't have a whole lot. I don't know his entire story inside and out, but let's just say that he was dealt a tough hand to play in the game of life. He didn't enroll in honors or AP courses. He didn't make good grades. He didn't play sports. He wasn't involved in any extracurricular activities. Brad was not a discipline problem, but he wasn't a kid that you saw on your roll at the beginning of the semester and developed a sense of excitement for having in class. Essentially, Brad was your stereotypical invisible kid. He was there at school, but nobody really knew him or what he was all about.

At the end of each school year, we meet with seniors that are borderline for fulfilling all of their requirements for graduation. Some of them need to score high on their final exam in a particular course that semester, some of them need to stay after school to complete online versions of courses that they previously failed, and some of them simply need a "hail Mary" to have a chance at walking across the stage.

That particular year, Brad was in the group of students in this meeting. As I addressed the group and attempted to encourage them by explaining the importance of graduation and the game-changer that a diploma can be in their life, I could tell that Brad was listening, but he showed absolutely zero emotion. No head nods, no moments of reflection, no acknowledgments, nothing.

That next month, Brad walked across the stage and received his diploma. Long after the ceremony was over, my bride and I walked out of the venue to a nearly empty parking lot. As we pulled out of the parking lot, I glanced over at a couple standing outside a car nearby. It was Brad and Samantha. I drove their way and rolled the window down to tell them both congratulations and tell them how proud I was of them.

Then, totally unprovoked, Brad asked me to get out of the car so that we could take a picture together. He thanked me and told me that he would have never walked across that stage if I hadn't spoken to that group of kids a month earlier.

> *He explained that for the first time in his life, it seemed as if somebody actually cared about him as a person.*

That conversation was one of the first times that our potential impact as educators really sank in for me.

Bradley

Bradley was a young man that I had in class in one of my later years as a classroom teacher. By this point in my career, I had developed an affection for at-risk youth as well as a pretty good track record of connecting with them. Bradley would prove to be one of my biggest challenges yet.

It was easy to tell that Bradley came from nothing. He placed no value whatsoever on grades or education, which is normally a seed planted at home. He ran with a rough, rough group of kids and was a frequent flyer in the office for disciplinary issues. Needless to say, he was not someone that you were excited to see on your class roster either.

I spent weeks and weeks trying to connect with Bradley. Nothing worked. He would make small talk, but I couldn't get to the breakthrough conversation. One of the biggest signs of success in reaching a kid in my experience is if they will willingly acknowledge you in the halls between classes when they are with their peers. Bradley would nod his head back at me, but that was all. All the while, I'm sure he was hoping his group of "friends" wouldn't notice, as this is often viewed as a sign of weakness for some reason.

A little over halfway through the semester, Bradley received out-of-school suspension. When I inquired as to the cause, I found out that he had missed detention and, because he had so many disciplinary infractions already, the next step was suspension. Upon his return to school, I asked him why he skipped detention and a mere 50 minutes of "punishment" in exchange for out-of-school suspension. He explained that his only mode of transportation to and from school was to ride the bus, so he literally had no choice other than to skip detention.

The next day, after spending the previous night reflecting on the situation, I told Bradley that from that point forward, any time he gets detention to let me know and I'll give him a ride home. There's no point in getting further behind in school and facing truancy issues over a 50-minute detention. He looked at me with an expression of bewilderment on his face and simply said, "thanks."

At that point, I had him. He started opening up to me a little bit more in our conversations. He started coming to school on a more regular basis. He started staying awake in class and, on most days, he actually put forth the effort to complete his work. Hook, line, and sinker, I had set the hook on Bradley.

About two weeks later, on a Monday, he didn't come to school. It turned out that over the weekend, Bradley was at a local park with his crew and got into a huge fight. The police were called and Bradley was one of the few people still there when they arrived. He was arrested, charged, and booked into juvenile detention.

[*That was the last time I saw Bradley. I had him… and I lost him.*]

I think about kids like Bradley every single day. Did I do enough? Could I have said something just a little bit different?

Could I have handled a situation differently? Did they know how much I cared? Did they know how much time I spent thinking about them? Did they know how badly I wanted to see them defeat the odds and succeed?

Kids like Bradley haunt my mind because no matter how many kids we save, there will always be those kids that got away. In all honesty, I think about those kids more than any of the others.

The moral of this story is that as much as we try and as much as we want to, we can't save them all. We are going to fail. As an educator, that can be hard to grasp and even harder to accept. But we can never stop trying.

Patrick

Patrick was a freshman in the hands-down worst-behaving class that I have ever had the opportunity to work with. Those kids were hell bent on creating disruption and chaos on a daily basis, and Patrick was the ringleader. He was obnoxiously loud, inappropriate, and talked nonstop regardless of what was going on in the classroom.

I despised this kid and the entire class. Why wouldn't they pay attention to my instructions and do as I asked? Why wouldn't they complete their assignments? Why wouldn't they follow the rules and guidelines that I had clearly laid out on the first day of school through a well-written syllabus? Why were they intent on ruining my day, each and every single day? Looking back now, the answer is simple: I was a horrible teacher at that point in time.

But then one day, I had an idea. I was "teaching" a lesson on conflict management and how to deal with different personalities. Knowing that Patrick was confrontational at even the slightest inclination, I devised a plan to use him as a key instrument in my lesson. Prior to class starting, I pulled him aside and nervously asked him to participate in my master scheme. His eyes lit up with excitement as he agreed to play his role.

As class started, I began speaking to the class about the plan of attack for the day. As per the usual, Patrick started talking out loud and interrupting my dialogue to the rest of the class. This led to a full blown argument with both of us yelling at one another until I finally yelled at him to leave the classroom. He obliged, and as we continued to argue back and forth, I followed him into the hall and slammed the door closed behind me.

About 10 seconds later, we opened the door and entered the dead silent classroom together, both of us with huge smiles on our faces. I immediately began explaining conflict resolution techniques and how the example that Patrick and I had just performed was a perfect example of how NOT to handle confrontation. Primarily because they were still in shock as to the prank we had just pulled, the class was more engaged that day than any day they had been up until that point in the school year.

Patrick, and that entire class for that matter, taught me a lot about teaching that year. Once I got Patrick to be on my side, the entire dynamic of my classroom changed. Point being, you have to find a way to connect with your students, especially those that have absolutely no desire to learn whatsoever. If you can find a way to get the ringleader to believe in what you are trying to do, your chances for success in the classroom dramatically increase.

> *Patrick taught me that kids don't want to meet me where I am. Instead, they want me to meet them where they are.*

That's a powerful, powerful concept that completely revolutionized my outlook both as an educator and as a person.

Peaches

Peaches was one of those kids that I will never forget for as long as I live. She was loud, almost to the point of being obnoxious, rambunctious, and carefree. She had one of those smiles that will absolutely light up a room. She also came with a reputation of being a "bad kid." She got in trouble on a regular basis and wasn't afraid to "throw hands" at the drop of a hat.

When I saw her name on my class roster that year, I knew I had two choices: I could turn it into a battlefield and attempt to get her in enough trouble that she would be sent to alternative school, or I could attempt to befriend her and have the "troublemaker" of the class on my side.

Fortunately for me, Peaches didn't give me much of an opportunity to decide. She entered my classroom with that monster smile of hers and never looked back. She was fun, upbeat, and almost always in a good mood. More important, for whatever reason, she loved me.

Peaches was one of the first kids to ever give me one of her senior pictures just before she graduated from high school.

This was before the kids started getting the fancy cards that have multiple pictures and quotes on them, so it was simply a wallet-size picture of her. On the back, she wrote a note thanking me for believing in her. After I read it, I gave her a big hug and said, "No ma'am...thank YOU for believing in me." I still have that picture to this day.

Cordell

Cordell transferred into our high school midway through the school year. He was a tall, skinny kid with gauges in both ears. You could tell at first glance that he wasn't going to find it easy to "fit in" in our rural, blue-collar community.

Cordell was a senior and he was up-to-date on his class credits, so he qualified for a class that we offered called Senior Project. During this class, seniors have one block of the day to work off campus for a local business or to work on campus for a teacher of their choice. Since Cordell was new to the community, he didn't have any business contacts and, since I taught Senior Project and he didn't know any teachers either, he asked if he could work for me. I, of course, said yes.

Cordell showed up for about a week and a half and never had much to say. He was perfectly content sitting in the back corner of the room with his headphones on, minding his own business, despite my valiant attempts at making conversation. But then, he stopped showing up to school.

Our community was very transient, so it was not uncommon for students to come and go on a fairly regular basis. This being known, I didn't make the time to go and check on Cordell to see if he had actually moved or what was going on with his particular situation. About a week or so later, I was driving home from school one afternoon and noticed Cordell walking home along the sidewalk with his backpack on. He had been at school that day, but he wasn't in my class.

In my early years as an educator, my only focus would have been to make an example of this young man. He had obviously skipped my class and had been doing so for quite some time, and he would have to pay! But at this point in my career, I had much greater intentions with my influence as an educator.

I pulled over and picked him up and gave him a ride home. On the way there, I didn't ask where he had been or talk about anything related to school. Instead, we just talked about life and shot the breeze until we pulled up to his home. This routine repeated itself for a few days in a row before finally I said to him one day on the ride home, "Cordell, I'm not mad at you at all, and you're not in trouble, but I just need to know where you're going during Senior Project. Are you going to shoot ball down in the gym? Are you going to another teacher's classroom? I just need to know where you are during that time period."

After a lengthy pause, he replied, "I didn't think I could tell anyone this, but my mom is a meth addict and she recently relapsed." He went on to explain to me that he was leaving school during Senior Project to walk home and check on his mom to make sure that she hadn't overdosed from the night before. Literally, he was ensuring that his mom was still alive. He then walked back to school in time for his next class and the remainder of his core academic classes throughout the day.

Talk about a reality check.

> *So often, as educators and especially as administrators, we want to see things in black and white. The truth is, however, that most of us cannot even begin to fathom how many shades of gray there are in our kids' lives.*

The last time I saw Cordell walking, he was in full graduation regalia, walking across the stage to shake our principal's hand as his name was called to receive his diploma. Does that piece of paper change the reality of the situation that he has to go home to every afternoon? No, it does not. But does it give him an opportunity to create a better tomorrow for himself and his future family? You better believe it does.

Cordell taught me once again that so many of our kids are faced with horrendous circumstances that are completely beyond their control.

Elizabeth

I had Elizabeth in class when she was a freshman. Shy, quiet, and kind would adequately describe her persona. Elizabeth was a great kid, but she never had much to say. She wasn't one of the "cool kids" by any stretch of the imagination, but she fit in well with her peers. She was in the marching band, so she naturally had a musical family to call her own.

I never had Elizabeth in class again after her freshman year, but I would see her frequently in the halls between classes. I would always smile and wave and tell her hello, to which she would return the favor.

As our senior class prepares to graduate each year, we hold a "senior week" during their last week of school as a way of honoring them and celebrating this milestone in their life. The week culminates with a staffulty talent show, during which adults in the building perform for the soon-to-be graduates. At the conclusion of the show, the seniors have the opportunity to write as many thank-you notes as they would like to write to any educator that influenced their life.

I have been beyond fortunate to receive a number of these thank-you notes, but the most powerful message that I ever received came on the note I received from Elizabeth. At the end, it read, "Thank you for always smiling and waving at me in the hall...it made me feel like I'm not invisible."

Not gonna lie, I cried. I still get teary-eyed just thinking about it. As educators, we spend so much of our time worrying about lesson plans and state standards and testing and other monotonies of the profession. As Elizabeth taught me, however, some of the most powerful things we can ever do have absolutely nothing to do with our subject matter and don't even take place in our classroom.

[*Sometimes, it really is as simple as a smile and a wave.*]

Juan

I honestly have no idea how my relationship with Juan began. I never had him in class. In fact, I don't think he ever even had a class in a room near mine. But for whatever reason, we connected.

Juan is a sports fanatic. He loves his Tennessee Titans, his Nashville Predators, and, more than anything else, he loves his

Portland High School Panthers. Juan was one of those kids that struggled to remember a scientific formula or the theme of a literature passage, but he could reel off statistics from sporting events in a heartbeat. From the NFL draft to junior varsity high school basketball, he knew who was doing what and how well they were doing it. He was at every single Portland High School athletic event, from Friday night football to volleyball matches and everything in between. He couldn't afford the price of admission, so he would often work for the team handing out programs or setting up the court or field in exchange for his entry fee.

Juan lived in a horrible environment. He was in and out of foster care during his younger days, resulting in him and his brother attending multiple different schools. Luckily, they were able to settle in at Portland High School for his sophomore, junior, and senior years. Even still, his home life was indescribable.

His family moved from place to place on a frequent basis, likely due to evictions. I am fairly certain that their home didn't have heat or air conditioning. I question if they had running water, because Juan and his brother both carried one of the most disgusting stenches that I have ever smelled in my life. Some kids, especially teenage boys, stink from time to time and get made fun of at school as they figure out the whole deodorant thing. This smell was beyond even that.

Juan and his brother rode their bikes to and from school every single day. When it was hot. When it was cold. When it was raining. When it was snowing. Regardless of the weather, if they were at school, it was because they woke up on their own and got themselves to school.

Again, I have no idea how we ever connected in the first place, but every day in the hall between classes, there he was, talking sports with me and the other people in my area. As I began to dig a little deeper into his story, we developed a bond that only grew stronger over the years. He had an affection for my college alma mater, Middle Tennessee State University, so I often took him with me to football and basketball games. I often picked him up and gave him a ride to our high school athletic events as well.

One of the most influential occurrences I had with Juan came during one of our trips to see an MTSU basketball game. I picked him up to head out on our hour-and-a-half trek, stopping at Chick-Fil-A along the way. He destroyed his lunch in a manner that I can't even explain. Then, later that day, we went out for supper at a Mexican restaurant. He and I both ordered a monster burrito, stuffed with grilled chicken and covered in queso. I found myself simply staring at him as he hovered over his plate and shoveled in bite after bite of his food.

He was starving. Literally, starving.

There are so many things that our kids experience that I can't even fathom...but I have done my best to understand their strife any way that I can. I frequently skip meals, partially because I'm busy, but more so because I want to better understand and relate to the feeling of hunger and what many of our students experience on a regular basis. I encourage you to try it at some point in time, even if it's just once...I guarantee it will provide you with a different perspective.

There were countless times that I felt like I literally had to drag Juan toward that graduation stage, but in May of 2016, that young man graduated from Portland High School. I rejoice in all of my students' successes, but Juan's was a little bit sweeter based on the circumstances and the time that we had invested in each other. Juan still has a long, long way to go to create a better life for himself, but I'm beyond proud to say that he is well on his way to doing just that.

Miguel

Juan's younger brother by two years, Miguel was even smaller than Juan. In fact, when I first saw Miguel, I thought he was one of the other educator's kids that had entered the building after their day at a local elementary school — he was that small.

From the first time Miguel entered my room until the last, he came in going 1,000 miles per hour and talking nonstop — so much so that it was difficult for me to get a word in edgewise. It was as if we had known each other all of our lives, the way that he would come in and talk about his day or a game or something new he had learned about on his phone.

Miguel's nickname was "Fire." When I asked him about it, he said that he loved fire because of the way the flames constantly bounce around. "You never know what they're going to look like and no two flames are ever alike, just like me," he explained to me. From that, I gave him the moniker of "Fireball," which he seemed to be pleased with.

Fireball, just like his older brother, struggled with a horrendous smell to his person. While his brother was much more reluctant, however, Fireball developed a system of bringing his clothes to me to be washed at school. He would drop them off in my room in the morning, I washed them during the day, and then he picked them up in the afternoon.

And then one day, I received a text message from the "father figure" at Fireball's home instructing me to stop doing his laundry because he "had it under control." I took this opportunity to invite the gentleman to school to discuss some important things regarding Juan and Fireball. He replied that he would check his schedule to see if he had time to come speak with me, despite the fact that he didn't have a job.

We never had that meeting, but you can bet that I kept washing those clothes.

Fireball struggled academically. My initial opinion of this was that it was due to a lack of cognitive ability, but I soon found that premise to be false. Fireball created a series of YouTube videos that detailed things you can do with your phone that absolutely blew my mind.

> *This young man wasn't a slow learner at all; simply put, school as we teach it wasn't useful to him, and he treated it as such.*

In April of 2017 as my family was preparing for bed, my bride saw a notification that a person had been struck by a train in our hometown. People walk all over town on a regular basis, so as much as I hated to hear this dreadful news, I didn't give it a lot of thought prior to falling asleep that night. The next morning, however, my bride was adamant that I get in touch with Juan and Fireball to make sure that they were okay. That's when I got the news from Juan…

It was Fireball.

I will always question if I did enough for Fireball. Did he know how much I loved him? Did he know how much I cared? Did he know how badly I wanted him and his brother to break the cycle of their childhood? There's a part of me that knows that Fireball is better off this way as opposed to the cruelty of life that he had to endure, but that doesn't take away the pain of what might have been. As much as I want to believe that I can save each and every single kid, in this case, I failed…and instead, a train was sent to do what I could not.

Part IV: See, Hear, Love

So, how do you do it? How do you truly make an impact with at-risk youth and give them a sense of hope for a better tomorrow? How do you inspire kids to pursue a greater purpose and passion?

For me, the answer comes in the form of another question: How do you NOT do it?

> *The greatest thing about being an educator is that each and every single day, we have the opportunity to make an immeasurable impact on tomorrow.*

Let that sink in for a minute.

Legendary leaders have the innate ability to inspire the hopeless and empower the dreamers.

So, how do you not do it? How do you not get fired up to work with your kids every day? How do you not get excited to put your thumbprint on a better tomorrow? No other profession on the planet gets to make those claims. How do you not do it?

One of our biggest weapons in making an impact comes with our mentality. In life, and in education especially, so many of the things that we do are because "that's the way it's always been done." Guys, that has to stop! No, we don't need to think outside the box...we need to blow the stupid box up! So it starts with shifting our mentality and being willing to try to implement new things in our approach toward teaching.

Be real.

With a focus on reaching at-risk youth, arguably the most important thing you have to understand is that you have to be real. These kids can see right through each and every single one of us. If you're not genuine in your actions and in your words, you've lost before the game even starts. Learn to be real with your kids, in your dress, your words, and your actions.

Generally speaking, as a profession, educators tend to "dress up" for work every day with the exception of a "casual Friday" or something similar. Have you ever stopped to ask yourself why we do that? Where and when did that start? And what purpose does it serve?

Imagine this scenario, if you will: You are an "at-risk" student on the first day of school. You come from an extremely poor family where food is scarce, shelter is a fluid place, and love is a foreign concept. As your teacher enters the room, they are dressed to the nines…guys in shirts and ties, fancy dress shoes, and designer watches; ladies in business suits or high heels with glamorous jewelry.

What is your first impression?

"They don't know me. They don't understand me. They don't know my struggle. They don't know about my story, nor do they care. They're privileged. They have no idea what it's like to live my life. They're just like all the others."

Those are not my words. Those are the words of at-risk students. How do I know that? Because I asked them myself. Often professions of all kinds get caught up in learning from "experts" in the field that spew their opinions based on their research and data calculations. The truth is, however, I can make the data say anything I want it to say in order to benefit my argument.

So for me, when I made it my mission to help students that are labeled as at-risk be successful, I didn't rely on any "experts" in the field or statistical data. Instead, I went straight to the source. I sat down, both individually and in groups, with these young men and women and had honest, real conversations with them. Those were their answers.

From that point forward, I never wore a tie again. I wore tennis shoes almost exclusively, sometimes mixing in some Chuck Taylor's. I frequently wore T-shirts and almost always wore my shirt untucked. Sometimes I even went as far as to wear a bandana or a hat to work and, on rare occasions, I even turned my hat around backward.

My relationships with and perception from the kids immediately flourished. Now, instead of being an overdressed, out-of-touch educator, I dressed much more in alignment with my personal brand and, in the process, made myself much more relatable to the kids…all of the kids. In reflecting on it now, it's not rocket science, and yet so many of us are dressed to the nines every single day to impress each other instead of servicing and marketing to our clientele, which always and forever will be, the students.

[
If you want to relate to your students, be it at-risk students or high-achieving students or anything in between, you have to make yourself relatable. It's literally that simple.
]

When I became a principal, I worked closely with a group of veteran educators that did not approve of my approach. Every time I walked into a meeting with them, they would all look me up and down from head to toe to evaluate my outfit that day. On multiple occasions, they would inform me that my dress wasn't "professional" and offered suggestions of what to wear and to "always carry a suit coat with me everywhere I go."

No thanks.

This profession is not, nor will it ever be, a fashion show. It's about changing lives, saving lives, and providing our students with the hope of a better tomorrow. If that means being judged by other educators in order to make a real and meaningful impact on the lives of my students, then so be it.

[*Make every decision with the best interest of your students in mind and you will never go wrong.*]

You have to be willing to be real with your words and conversations as well.

Make yourself vulnerable and share yourself.

How do you relate to your kids? You have to be willing to make yourself vulnerable, which includes sharing stories of your personal failures and struggles. So often, educators are viewed by students as these angelic-type characters, when in reality, each and every single one of us has a story of struggle and hardship that we have had to overcome. In fact, many of us experience struggles and hardships in life that we have to overcome throughout our present life status.

Be willing to share these experiences with your students. No, you don't have to go into great detail and share each and every single little part of your situation, but be willing to put the general concept out there. When your students see you as a real person as opposed to a stereotypical educator, the pathway to meaningful connections becomes much less muddied.

I'm adopted. I'm divorced. I've been in trouble with the law for consuming alcohol as a minor. I've been fired. I've made errors on the baseball field that cost my team the game. I've made bad decisions as a father. I've made bad decisions in my career choices. I've had a speeding ticket. I've forgotten my best friend's birthday.

I have failed over and over again in all aspects of my life.

My students know about all of those things. I share them openly and use them as what I hope to be teachable moments. I make myself vulnerable so that my kids will see and understand that failure is a part of life. The difference between winning and losing is not in how many times you fail, but instead how you react to and learn from your failures.

Hopefully, the stories of my past personal failures have impacted the futures of my kids.

Identify their needs.

Actions always speak louder than words, as the cliché goes, and this is never truer than in making connections with at-risk youth. These kids see straight through our words and the pretty picture that most of us paint through our dialogue and instead focus directly on our actions. What do you actually *do* that makes a difference?

Before you can actually do anything to help your kids, you have to identify their needs. This can only be accomplished through establishing meaningful relationships and connections so that not only can you develop a greater understanding of what they are all about, but they can also build and develop a level of trust and belief that you are genuinely concerned about their best interest. Then, and only then, will they make themselves susceptible to you playing an active role in their lives.

On the first day of school, create a short questionnaire for your students to complete. In addition to the usual contact info that all first-day questionnaires ask for, include questions that provide you with insights into what your students are all about. Be sure to include things like their favorite musical artist or band, their social media handles, their hobbies and interests, their favorite fast food restaurant, their favorite athlete and sports teams, and so on. Because it's the first day of school and most students are on their best behavior, they are more likely to actually complete this form and provide meaningful information for you on this day than on any other.

Once you have these completed forms, now YOU have a homework assignment — study the information your kids have provided! As soon as the next opportunity presents itself, use tidbits of the information provided to create conversations with your kids. "Hey, I saw where you're a Cowboys fan, I love them too!" Or, "That's so cool that you love to draw, can I see some of your work?" All of a sudden, you've made an effort to take an interest in their personal life and, as sad as it sounds, many of our kids never get that kind of attention in their lives.

To take this a step further, use the information you have learned and then take the time to study it further. For example, check out their favorite musical artist or band on YouTube and see what they are all about, even if it is a genre of music that you don't particularly care for. Find at least a song or a couple of lines from a song that stand out to you and then use that to spark a conversation with that student.

If you really want to take it to the next level, the next time you're out shopping, pick up a hat or a piece of clothing that has their favorite team or musical artist on it. "I was out yesterday and when I saw this, it made me think of you." All of a sudden, not only did you take the time to learn about something that they like in their personal life, but you also put forth the effort to invest in them as well.

Find ways to position your students for success.

From there, find ways to put your kids in positions to be successful. This means that you'll have to take some chances along the way and provide opportunities for them that the majority of the other educators in your building would never dream of, but remember: average educators are soon to be forgotten.

> *We are here to leave a legacy of hope and love, and this can only be done through the framework of strategic risks and the belief that all kids genuinely want to do good and to be good at their core.*

Maybe it starts with asking them to run a simple errand for you during the school day to the front office or to another teacher's classroom. From there, find a project or two that you want completed and find a way to get them involved. I once asked three "outcast" students to help paint our picnic tables for an outdoor eating area we were constructing, and they loved doing it! Not only that, but it gave them *ownership* in our school, and that's a huge piece of making connections with kids. Because they were involved in that project, do you think that they, or any of their friends, ever considered defacing that property? Not in a million years!

I once had a young man who was extremely talented at graffiti — I discovered this through a note that he left for me in the restroom one day! However, we took that negative situation and turned it into something positive through the use of his talent. I asked that young man to tag "Don't stop believing," our school's yearly mantra, on a wall in our front hallway. All of a sudden, that "outcast" of a young man had ownership in our building and I had a positive connection that I could build on from that point forward.

Understand and use social media to connect with students.

One of the greatest resources to take advantage of in terms of building relationships with your students is social media. Get connected with your kids on social media! I cannot emphasize enough how beneficial this will prove to be in so many different regards. If you don't understand how social media or a particular social media platform works, ASK YOUR KIDS! Not only are they already experts, but this presents yet another opportunity for you to interact with them on a topic outside of the realm of school.

Social media allows you to make a personal connection with your students and provides a direct window into their lives. Kids, and adults for that matter, post EVERYTHING on social media! It serves as a great resource to learn more about their interests and what they are all about as people. In addition, it also often provides a look inside their living conditions and the values that they have been taught throughout their childhood. Every little piece of information you can gather plays a huge role in establishing and nurturing those relationships!

From a big picture perspective, social media provides you with the opportunity to keep your finger on the pulse of the climate of your school. I cannot begin to count how many situations I learned about, both good and bad, simply by scrolling through social media. This provides you with the opportunity to diffuse situations before they escalate and become something much bigger than they ever need to be.

Social media also provides another opportunity for your kids to see you as a real person as opposed to the stereotypical teacher myth that they all seem to have in their minds. You actually do have a life outside of the classroom? No way! You went to a concert? Or a ballgame? AND you know how to take a selfie?!? Mind = blown! But in all seriousness, use this opportunity to connect with your students...it will only help you in the long run.

In addition to sharing your personal stories on social media, make sure that you are sharing your school's story as well! There are unbelievable things that happen in our schools each and every single day. As educators, we must do a better job of sharing the positive with our stakeholders! People, young and old alike, are constantly on their phones, so what better avenue to use than social media to tell your school's story?

Explore reasons for poor attendance.

At-risk students are often susceptible to poor attendance at school for various reasons, many of which are often beyond their control. If you have a student that has been absent for two or three days in a row, shoot them a private message through social media and check in on them. "Hey, we've missed you in class these past few days. If you need anything, let me know!" All of a sudden, you took the time out of your day to check on their well-being. I don't have the words to explain to you how much that means to so many of these kids.

Identify things they need.

How else can you connect with your at-risk students? Start by identifying things that they need. This might be as simple as a pen or a pencil or a notebook filled with paper. Again, so many of their adult supporters either don't have the resources to provide these things or they don't have the interest in providing them, so oftentimes the kids are left to fend for themselves for even the simplest of school supplies.

Instead of taking all of your "old" clothes to goodwill or having a yard sale, bring them to school and let your kids in need have the opportunity to take what they want. If you have a student that is in need but doesn't wear your size, find a way to make it happen. Seek out another person in your building and ask them if they have any old clothes or shoes they are looking to get rid of. Many of our youth wear the same clothes multiple times in the same week because that's all they have. Identify their needs, and then create solutions. That's leadership.

Many at-risk youth need assistance with washing their clothes and hygiene because they aren't afforded those luxuries at home. Provide a resource for them to get this accomplished. Almost every school has a washing machine and dryer in their building, be it for a family and consumer science class or for athletics. Bring a jug of laundry detergent and dryer sheets to school and store them in your office. Tell your kids to bring you their clothes in the morning and that you will have them washed and dried by that afternoon…and then do it.

One of the most difficult conversations I have ever had to have in my entire life took place with Juan and Fireball. As previously mentioned, they both had one of the most horrendous stenches associated with their presence that I have ever smelled in my entire life. Do you have any idea how difficult it is to tell someone that they stink? There is not a person on this planet that ever wants to hear those words, let alone impressionable, teenage boys.

> [*Changing lives means that sometimes you have to have the difficult conversations.*]

Create a desk drawer filled with hygiene items like toothbrushes and toothpaste, deodorant, combs, and the like. Make sure that your kids know where it is located and its contents and then give them free reign to take things as needed. DO NOT make the mistake of giving them supplies in front of their peers! Nobody wants to be seen in that light, so make sure that you take every step necessary to preserve the integrity and pride of your students that you are attempting to help.

Help with transportation.

Transportation is often a huge obstacle for at-risk youth, so offer to help them out with a ride any time you can. At an early stage in my tenure at one high school, I noticed that a lot of my kids were receiving out of school suspension despite the fact that they hadn't been in any "big trouble" that I was aware of. When I started asking the kids what happened, they told me that they received detention for something trivial (usually being late to class). Because their only mode of transportation to and from school was the bus, however, they couldn't stay after school to serve detention. As a result, their punishment escalated from a simple hour-long detention session to out of school suspension.

The topic of discipline deserves its own standalone dialogue in and of itself, but how is out of school suspension going to benefit these kids with regard to their education? Point blank, it doesn't. So, how can we remedy this situation?

Be their transportation. Seriously. When I found out what was going on, I thought I was going to lose my mind! From that point forward, I made sure that my kids knew that if they messed up and got detention, they were to let me know about it and I will give them a ride home after serving their hour of punishment.

There is absolutely no need for a mundane infraction to turn into something that keeps them away from their greatest opportunity of breaking out of the lifestyle from which they come!

Transportation doesn't have to be limited to this situation, either. In order for kids to feel connected to their school, they have to be involved. Not only should you invite them to attend extracurricular activities, but also offer to give them a ride to the ballgame or the play that's taking place at school. Want to take it to the next level? Swing through McDonald's and order them a sandwich or chicken nuggets on the way. So many of the things that most of us take for granted are a rare occurrence for our kids. Show them what can happen through the power of love and education!

Be available to them.

I give all of my students, and any student that asks or that I interact with at all, my personal cell phone number. You need me? Call me. You need a ride? Text me. You're having trouble at school? I want to know about it so I can help. You need a tie to wear during graduation? I'll bring you one. Essentially, I attempt to break down all of the barriers to potential excuses on day one.

Is this an unconventional approach? Yes. I never had any of my teachers' phone numbers, not even my coaches. But then again, I didn't need them because I had parents at home that provided for me.

Unconventional circumstances call for unconventional solutions.

> *Beyond the walls of your classroom or office, remember that every single time you pass a student in the hallway, you are constructing the school climate. Whether you are building it up or tearing it down depends on you.*

Know their names and greet them.

Regardless of the one million things going through your mind at the moment, smile, wave, and say hello. Create eye contact. Not just sometimes, but Every. Single. Time. Even with the kids that you don't like.

In addition, learn as many names of the students in your building as humanly possible and then call them by their name when you see them in the hallway. Want to blow a kid's mind? Call a student by name that you've never had in class, in your club, or on your team.

Don't know their names? No problem! Grab a yearbook, then every week, challenge yourself to learn the names of five new faces that you aren't familiar with. Social media can help with putting names with faces as well. Take advantage of all the resources you have available to better relate to your kids!

The vast majority of this book focuses on establishing and nurturing relationships, but your instructional pedagogy plays a tremendous role as well. It is important to note, however, that without a developed rapport with your kids, even the greatest teaching methods in the world will be for not with many of our nation's youth. As the late, great Rita Pierson stated, "Kids don't learn from people they don't like."

Understand on the front end that adapting your teaching methods will take time, creativity, innovation, and continual efforts to stay up to date with modern day happenings. In order to connect with kids, all kids, we have to be in tune with pop culture and social media and what is going on in *their* lives. Simply put, if you're not up to speed with *their* worlds, you're out of touch, and if you're out of touch, you need to get out of education. Plain and simple.

Use music and pop culture.

There's not a better way to set the tone for the climate of your classroom or office than with music. Every single day, make sure that you have a playlist going as students enter and exit your classroom. Make sure that you include a variety of music in an effort to appease the tastes of as many different people as possible, but maintain a focus on modern day pop music.

Administrators, music can play a key role for you as well. For starters, just like a teacher's classroom, it sets the tone for visitors that enter your office. If you want to take music to the next level, have it played in your hallways during class breaks. Again, the goal here is to create a fun, energetic environment, and who doesn't love music? You wanna see something fun? Imagine students and staff members doing the Cha-Cha Slide in the hall between classes — now THAT'S fun!

Find and use ways to incorporate pop culture into your lessons. Maybe there is a reality show that you can correlate to a review game you are going to play; maybe there is a popular song that you can "remix" to create lyrics that convey your lesson for the day; maybe there is a hit movie that utilizes a plot that relates to a topic you are covering in a particular unit. Whatever the case may be, find ways to bring modern day trends into your classroom on a daily basis.

See them. Hear them. Love them. Every day.

At the end of the day, it's about seeing our kids. It's about hearing our kids. And, it's about loving our kids. I always ask educators, if you don't genuinely love each and every single one of your kids, then why are you in this profession? Seriously. And I don't mean just the "honor kids" or just the "good kids" or the "leadership kids" that we all want the chance to work with. I mean genuinely, passionately, and relentlessly love ALL kids.

Are you going to have bad days? Yeah, you are. Are there going to be lessons that crash and burn and fail miserably? You bet there are. Are there going to be days where you don't feel well and you would rather just stay home? No doubt there will be. Will there be times that, despite your best effort, you feel like you are isolated on an island and nobody understands how much you care and how badly you want to help? Unfortunately, this is true as well.

But again, I ask each of you, why did you enter this great profession in the first place? Without being there to hear your answers, I can still guarantee you this: not a single one of you answered that question with mediocrity in mind. Not a single educator enters this field to maintain the status quo. Not a single educator becomes a teacher to simply be average. And not a single one of us enter this career to be forgotten.

Again, the single greatest thing about being an educator is that each and every day, we have the opportunity to make an immeasurable impact on tomorrow.

Take a moment to process what that statement really means to you. Think about the tremendous value that you bring to the world. Think about how your ability to reach our youth literally has the potential to change family trees. Education matters, teachers matter, and you matter.

My challenge to each of you is this: Every single day when you pull into that parking lot at your school, regardless of how you feel, the day of the week, the weather outside, what's going on in your personal life, regardless of everything else that the outside world throws at you — find a way to flip the switch and turn on that rock star educator that you entered this career field to become in the first place. Unleash your passion and energy and make a difference in the lives of your kids. Be relentless in your pursuit of success. Your kids deserve it, your colleagues deserve it, and, most important, you deserve it.

To each and every single person reading this, I want you to *feel* these three things from the bottom of my heart:

I see you.

I hear you.

And I love you.

Go be legendary.

Part V: Reflections

My goal in writing this book was not only to share my personal story and experiences, but also to provoke thought, dialogue, and reflection for the reader as well. For me personally, and from what I have gathered through conversations with educators across the country, we often replicate our teaching practice based on our own personal experiences as students. Furthermore, we also tend to lean toward our preferred learning style with our instructional pedagogy as opposed to what might be best for our students in today's classroom.

Hopefully, you experienced at least one "ah-ha" moment while reading this book. Whether that moment leads to a different approach with a student, a different method that you will employ in your instruction or a shift in your mindset toward education, I sincerely hope that it leads you to becoming a better educator as well as a better person.

One of the most important takeaways is that not all "at-risk" students fall under the stereotypical indicators. A student can live in a home with both biological parents and have all of their needs met and still fall under the category of "at-risk." My dear friend and fellow educator, Paul Dols, provides a great example of this in the foreword of this book through a brief summary his personal story. "At-risk" does not mean a certain socioeconomic status, a certain race or nationality, cognitive ability, or the neighborhood from which a student comes. "At-risk" means that a student believes that they are invisible, that they are a ghost, and that they are not seen, heard, or loved.

The remainder of this book is designed for reflection and personal growth. The questions are meant to provide the opportunity for you to analyze and evaluate not only where you have been as an educator, but more important, where you are going as an educator and ways you can expand the impact you make on the world.

While each question has its own page for you to write your personal thoughts on paper, this is certainly not a requirement. One of the most important aspects to growing as a person is knowing who you are and how you learn best. Some people need to write things down, while others simply need quiet "me time" to sort things out in their mind.

For me personally, my "me time" comes while I run. I can't begin to tell you how many problems I have solved or how many ideas I have formulated during my daily exercise routine. Regardless of your preferred method of learning, the important takeaway is that you make YOU a priority every single day…whether that is through writing, exercise, quiet time in the car on the way home from work in the afternoon, or any other method that you prefer.

Point being, broken hearts tend to be lonely…love yourself first, and then pour yourself into others.

1. What is your definition of "at-risk?" How do you identify students in your building that fall under this umbrella?

_____

_____

_____

_____

_____

_____

_____

_____

_____

_____

_____

_____

_____

_____

_____

_____

_____

2. Think about an "at-risk" student (or students) that you have had in the past. If you could go back and do something different, what would you change? Why?

3. What will you change about your personal approach to education that will lend itself to greater success with "at-risk" students moving forward?

4. Think about the first day of school in your classroom. What activities can you incorporate to establish meaningful relationships with your students? What about on a school-wide level?

_____

_____

_____

_____

_____

_____

_____

_____

_____

_____

_____

_____

_____

_____

5. How can you incorporate more of the "real world" into your classroom lessons in an effort to make it more meaningful and relatable to your students?

6. How are transfer students greeted at your school? How could this process be improved?

7. Do you have a default view of your students' adult supporters that is positive or negative, specifically with regard to your "at-risk" students? What strategies have you used to include them in the past and to understand their personal situations? What will you change about that approach moving forward?

_____

_____

_____

_____

_____

_____

_____

_____

_____

_____

_____

_____

_____

_____

8. Think about a disciplinary issue that you did not handle well. If you could go back and do it all over again, what would you change?

9. What types of activities can your school add to improve upon the overall climate of your building? Focus on the time periods before school starts, between classes, the lunchroom experience, and after school.

10. As students (and other stakeholders) enter and exit your campus, what do they see? What do they hear? How do they feel? Focus on all of your entrances and exits, but specifically on your bus lane. How can this experience be improved?

11. What can you do outside your classroom to reach "at-risk" youth? What about outside of regular school hours?

12. In what ways have you made yourself vulnerable and relatable to your students? How can you improve in this area moving forward?

13. If you haven't experienced poverty or hunger or the belief that you are invisible, what can you do to develop a greater understanding of where these kids are coming from?

14. In your personal experience, what educator has done the best job in reaching "at-risk" youth? In your opinion, what made them successful? Set up an hour of time to meet with them and discuss this topic.

_____

_____

_____

_____

_____

_____

_____

_____

_____

_____

_____

_____

_____

_____

_____

_____

15. Call to action: What are three things you are going to do to better meet the needs of "at-risk" students in your building?

About the Author

Dr. Phil Campbell, better known as PC, graduated from Riverdale High School in Murfreesboro, TN in 1997 prior to attending Middle Tennessee State University to play baseball. After graduating in 2001 with a degree in Agribusiness, PC volunteered as a baseball coach at a local high school and quickly fell in love with working with kids. As such, he returned to MTSU and earned his Master's Degree in Business Education so that he could teach and coach baseball. In doing so, he crossed paths with his future bride, Tara, and the two have been inseparable since. PC has 16 years of experience as a teacher, coach, athletic director, and principal. His expertise lies in leadership, motivation, reaching at-risk youth, and revolutionizing school culture and climate. PC resigned from education in 2016 and is now working as an educational speaker, consultant, and creative in addition to serving as an ambassador for Jostens Renaissance.

www.pcrocks.net
Twitter: @drphilcampbell
Instagram: @drphilcampbell
Facebook: @drphilcampbell
Snap: Doctor_PC